GET COACHED

15 inspiring stories from small business owners about how their journeys with a business coach helped to shape their success

ROBIN WAITE

Bestselling author of **Online Business Startup** and **Take Your Shot**

THE FEARLESS BUSINESS COACH

First Published in Great Britain 2018

By Robin M. Waite

Copyright © 2018 by Robin M. Waite

Paperback ISBN 978-0-9957768-4-5

Robin Waite Limited
Stroud House
Russell Street
Stroud
Gloucestershire
GL5 3AN

www.robinwaite.com

CONTENTS

For all of my Fearless Crew, without you I wouldn't have the best job in the world ~~Coaching~~ you amazing people. Thank you for all of your support.

INTRODUCTION

This isn't a sales pitch for Fearless Business, there, I've got my cheeky plug in...

But it is a sales pitch for all the amazing coaches around the world, from life coaches to business coaches and sales coaches to fitness coaches.

No matter what you are struggling with, everyone needs a coach. They're good enough for sports people, so why wouldn't they be good enough for the average, tired and frustrated business owner?

This is for you if you're struggling, feel like you've got more to give, maybe your business has plateaued, and you lie awake at night wondering where your next client is coming from.

You could be a narky, spoilt mess of a human being (externally) but internally, you're simply frustrated that you can't help all the 7+ billion people on the planet.

Maybe you feel your life is split, unequally, between work and family.

Your stress levels are soaring, you're constantly running around all over the place chasing all the balls you threw up in the air over the last few years...

But none of them are landing...

...maybe you need some help.

A coach can show up in any number of different ways.

It could be a business, life, sports or wellbeing coach.

It could also be a mentor, someone you look up to and respect.

An author, speaker or a book.

Your grandad who died years ago but still inspires you today. I often ask myself, "What would Dad think?"

Your wife, son, aunt or best man.

A good friend, who runs their own business who you can share ideas with and the odd rant.

Anyone can show up in life as a coach.

But first you must:

1. realise that life is pretty tough sometimes
2. admit that you need some help
3. ask for help...from anyone
4. accept their help

Take these steps and you stand a much greater chance of achieving success.

Keep on doing the same old thing? Well, you guessed it, nothing is ever going to change.

Replace can't, won't, never, always, should, shouldn't and all the other bullshit negative responses with, "I can!" and, "I am!" and your world will change forever. Quite often though we don't even know we're doing it. Your Dad, aunt, husband, wife, kids, suppliers, customers and your coach can all see you doing it, but you can't.

Subtly, I've just introduced the concept of The Yellow Car.

Don't know what that is?

Well, you don't notice yellow cars until you either buy one or start looking for them. When you do, you see the damned things everywhere.

So, now that I've warned you about some of the indicators that you might need a coach, YOU will start to identify them.

Get Coached isn't a load of woo-woo bullshit drivel from 'yet another coach'.

It is, a compilation of stories, from awesome human beings who have been coached, explaining what their hump was and how coaching helped them get over it.

Warts and all.

Simple!

Ok, here's the apology, I'm a Business Coach, so most of their stories are, well, businessey...sorry about that!!

They are, however, fascinating stories written by real people who have experienced what it is truly like to be coached.

I'll say again.

You don't NEED me, or any other coach for that matter. You

must WANT to be coached.

End of.

Enjoy the stories.

And when you're ready to be coached. *GET COACHED.*

CHAPTER 1

I'VE MANAGED BUSINESSES FOR 20 YEARS, WHY DO I NEED TO BE COACHED?

WHAT DO YOU FEEL WAS MISSING FROM YOUR BUSINESS BEFORE YOU ENGAGED A COACH?

There was very little automation within the business, so the client on-boarding process was inconsistent and time-consuming. I had lots of packages for lots of things, but they were mainly one-off jobs for a one-off payment.

I was always looking for new customers to keep the cash flow going.

I tried to do everything myself and used lots of applications and software that were free. Free in general not being efficient.

I did very little networking, and although I was getting a lot of enquires from Google, local people and businesses weren't aware of how I could help their business get found.

When I look back at it now, I realise that it wouldn't have been that long before I would have thrown in the towel and gone back to being employed again. It was chaotic and I wasn't making enough money for it to be sustainable in the long term.

WHAT WAS THE SHIFT THAT GOT YOU STARTED ON YOUR SELF-DEVELOPMENT JOURNEY?

I had already made changes after I had decided I wanted a "portable" business due to the Ill health of my father and that being tied to working from my office/photography studio I wanted to do any more. So I attended a seminar held by Robin in Jury's Hotel in Cheltenham, where I listened and listened. In a short time, it dawned on me that if I really wanted the business to succeed and to have the "portable" business I needed to be able to have the work/life balance my life needed right now, then something had to change. Everything that Robin said in that seminar resonated with me and I knew I had found the right person to help me to take my business to the next level and upwards from there.

WHAT MOMENT TRIGGERED YOU TO THINK, "I NEED TO DO SOMETHING DIFFERENT RIGHT NOW OTHERWISE NOTHING IS EVER GOING TO CHANGE."

I had a loan from the bank to purchase my new office to work from, however, I hadn't really planned out my journey from where I was to achieving the business I wanted. There were so many things I hadn't factored in.

I booked a breakthrough meeting with Robin where we discussed my business, my plans, what I wanted to achieve and what I had been doing.

I came from that meeting feeling like the world had been lifted off my shoulders with a clear plan of what I needed to do going forward with the ongoing support and challenges from Robin's Fearless Business programme.

WHAT'S THE 'ONE THING' YOU HAVE ACHIEVED THROUGH BEING COACHED?

Within 3 months I had my "portable" business. I was confident in the way forward, and the business was running more smoothly. I gained lots of new clients. This enabled me to spend quality time with my mother after my father passed away, whilst still being able to service my local SEO clients. For which I will always be truly thankful.

Since then the business has grown from strength to strength. I have now trebled my turnover within 6 months and I am now working with the clients I want to work with on a regular basis. No more pain in the arse clients that I had to take on because I needed the money.

I felt fantastic, excited, proud and clear about my vision of the future of my business.

I wish I had realised I needed a proper business coach from day 1 of setting up my business. There were lots of people giving me advice, mentors provided by the government, but their approach was generic and often the information given was incorrect.

COULD YOU HAVE DONE IT ON YOUR OWN?

In a word, NO. At that particular time, I had received two job offers and had signed a contract on one but not posted it. I felt I needed security and employment would feel secure. Being coached by Robin and being part of the Fearless Group has given me that security and confidence to grow my business and I have no plans in going back to being employed any time soon.

IF YOU COULD DELIVER YOURSELF A MESSAGE WHEN YOU FIRST STARTED YOUR BUSINESS WHAT WOULD IT BE?

"Get yourself a business coach, forget the fact you have managed businesses for over 20 years. Forget your background. Speak to someone who gets you and your business."

**Chris Attwood-Thomas, Think Local Seo
and Photography - thinklocalseo.co.uk**

Author's tip: Picking the right coach is tough, there are lots of us to choose from. In a first meeting, every word they say may resonate with you instantly, because the process of being listened to always creates an emotionally charged meeting. Follow up, find out more. Explore their background and content they share, to check they are who they say are. For coaching to succeed, the relationship has to fit you as a person as well as what your business needs.

CHAPTER 2
WINGING IT

WHAT DO YOU FEEL WAS MISSING FROM YOUR BUSINESS BEFORE YOU ENGAGED A COACH?

Renosash was started from a desire for our family to be more self-sufficient. To enable us to be less dependent on any one single individual or organisation. We wanted to provide home-owners with good quality workmanship for their sash windows. And we wanted to run our own schedule.

Chris had been self-employed for so long, sub-contracting for a local sash window company, that at first the business naturally began to run in a similar way. Chris was the core of the business, and I provided support and advertising ideas.

We started slowly bringing in different methods for the business that I had used during my engineering career. All with the aim that I could start taking some tasks from Chris to free him up. Overall, we were very much focused on the day to day running of the business and the system within.

But what mistakes were we making? So many!

We did what we needed to do, to ensure we had money coming

in to pay the bills. But we were not doing a great job of running a standalone business. It was an extension of Chris's self-employment. We had no real structure or organisation outside of Chris's head and I had no real job role, other than support.

So how do I feel about myself and the business then? I admit, I feel slightly ashamed that, even with my qualifications, of which business management was a part, that we actually ran our business with such a lack of structure, missing some of the basic business fundamentals. We were busy and had a young family also pulling on our time. We were firefighting with all the tasks that needed doing to keep the money coming in. But that's no excuse!

What was our greatest challenge? Thinking back, we had a number of challenges before we started using a coach. But our biggest two were time and value. There just wasn't enough time and we were seriously undervaluing the quality of our final product.

WHAT WAS THE SHIFT THAT GOT YOU STARTED ON YOUR SELF-DEVELOPMENT JOURNEY?

Short answer: We had a child, and then another one.

Longer answer: I had spent most of my working life in an engineering career (except a rebellious period where I tried my hand as a gym instructor/ personal trainer). When we had our first child we looked at the finances and decided that Chris should continue as a self-employed sub-contractor full-time, and I return to my engineering technician role part-time. It worked for a while, but eventually, the early mornings, the pressure to do more at work, and pressure from the company Chris sub-contracted for took its toll.

So we set up Renosash. This was step 1 in our development process.

How did it feel? Scary!

I had been employed for the whole of my working life since I was 15. Breaking away from that was a daunting prospect. But it was also liberating, exciting and full of potential. It gave us hope that we could lead a happy life, where we could spend more time with our young family.

Unfortunately, finding time for the business admin was much more difficult than we anticipated. The business continued to survive in Chris's head, which was often too focused on completing projects to a high standard and not focused enough on overall business admin and progression.

Our journey with a coach was a slow, gradual one rather than a lightbulb moment. We used his online videos, then read his book, went to a seminar and then used his online course, before we actually got round to seeing Robin for a one-to-one session. It was all of these things combined that enabled us both to see that using a coach would be a useful step for us. This was step 2.

WHAT'S THE 'ONE THING' YOU HAVE ACHIEVED THROUGH BEING COACHED?

Aside from the practical things that Robin tasked us with (a customer journey board, a new works inspection sheet, a new invoicing and estimating system), we have developed the confidence to try new methods and to give ourselves 'permission' to deviate from our current methods. His Fearless group has also given us challenges to complete which we would not have tried before (using social media videos for example).

On a personal level, it has made me look at my own role within the business. It has made me look at my life goals with a fresh perspective, and I have been working towards these with fresh enthusiasm.

Would I do anything differently?

I could kick myself for not seeing him sooner. I led myself to believe we couldn't see him as we were too busy. But actually, If I had just booked the session and gone, we would have started this journey 5 months earlier.

How did we overcome our major challenge? Our major challenge was time, and we are still working on finding a good balance. Mentally though, we have jumped the hurdle of believing we need to fit everything in, which was making life stressful before. Now we are in a place where we can accept that some things are going to slide, or we can get someone else to do some tasks so that we can concentrate on other things. A much healthier place for us to be in.

COULD YOU HAVE DONE IT ON YOUR OWN?

The simple answer to this is no. I knew the basics of running a business. I had completed with merits business management modules.

I had read business books, reports, and articles. But what nobody had said was that once you start working in your business, it is highly likely that you will neglect to work 'ON' your business.

A business coach gives you the outside perspective and reminds you to work on your business with some helpful prompts to guide you. Sometimes what you need is someone on the outside looking in to tell you where your next move is.

IF YOU COULD DELIVER YOURSELF A MESSAGE WHEN YOU FIRST STARTED YOUR BUSINESS WHAT WOULD IT BE?

"Write down your goals. For your business, your life, the year, the month. Re-visit them often. And work towards them every damn day. And if you lose your stride for a time, don't beat yourself up about it, just re-visit your goals and remember what you are working towards.

Get an outsider to help guide and prompt you. A coach or mentor will help you keep focus.

Be ambitious and aim higher than you think you should. It is only by being ambitious that great things are achieved!"

Sam Causon, Renosash - www.renosash.co.uk

Author's tip: Business owners who plan are more likely to succeed. Whether you believe the research or not, coaching will help you identify your goal and formulate your plans with greater clarity. Then you can move on more quickly to get shit done.

CHAPTER 3
TAKE THE LEAP

WHAT DO YOU FEEL WAS MISSING FROM YOUR BUSINESS BEFORE YOU ENGAGED A COACH?

I started my business because I had my daughter and was unable to go back to my HR role. I saw this as a bit of a blessing as I had always known I wanted to be self-employed but, like a lot of people, I was comfortable working for someone else and never had a defining moment when I was ready to take that risk. When I became a Mum I remember thinking, you're out of excuses now, if you don't do it now you'll regret it for the rest of your life. I totally understood then why it's called a 'window of opportunity' because I felt like if it closed again, I would never be able to open it.

My problem was, I had a lot of ideas but no clue how to put them into action. I was making endless lists but not doing anything with them. I felt really alone trying to juggle childcare of my daughter, running the house, undertaking a qualification and learning everything about starting up a business. I knew where I wanted to be, but I had no idea how to get there!

I had employed the strategy of 'just say yes' to every opportunity

I came across. It was wonderful for making connections and building on ideas but terrible for planning and keeping to any structure.

I always felt that I didn't have enough time, that I was running from one 'chore' to the next. I was feeling guilty about always thinking about work when I was with my daughter, especially as she was the whole reason I had decided to be self-employed in the first place!

I was at a point where I knew I had to do something or I'd have to climb back in the window. And I wasn't doing that.

WHAT WAS THE SHIFT THAT GOT YOU STARTED ON YOUR SELF-DEVELOPMENT JOURNEY?

As a coach myself, I was in a space where I thought about personal development a lot. I had a mentor through an organisation I was connected with and several more senior coaches had met me for coffee and shared their wisdom with me.

I always found the meetings really useful, but there was no follow up and I'd find myself off track again in a month's time.

I realised that it was consistent support from someone else that was going to be key to my success. Someone, not only to ask advice and use as a sounding board but also someone I could share my wins with in my business. It's pretty lonely working on your own and high-fiving the mirror when you get a new client!

The first coach I worked with completely understood my situation; she had set up a business herself around her children, we had the same values and outlook on life.

As soon as I signed up to work with her, I felt more confident, more organised and more serious about my business. I had made an investment in myself and it felt amazing!

WHAT'S THE 'ONE THING' YOU HAVE ACHIEVED THROUGH BEING COACHED

Since then I have worked with various coaches and all have given me something different and a new perspective.

There have been so many ways that a coach has made a difference, I organise my time differently, I changed my daughter's child care arrangements and eliminated (most of) the guilt. I really know how to prioritise now and keep my head down and focus on what I want to achieve rather than what other people are doing.

The biggest thing for me about coaching, which has been true with everyone I have worked with, is that it's about holding a space for you to think. It's difficult to do on your own because you get distracted or never get round to it, but when you have an appointment to sit with someone and really think and have them help you do that, it's really powerful. I always leave coaching sessions feeling more confident, energised and clearer about what's important.

COULD YOU HAVE DONE IT ON YOUR OWN?

I honestly don't think I could do it on my own. I know as a coach I'm bound to say that! But honestly, there have been times when I have worked without a Coach and I just haven't got as much done. Plain and simple.

When I don't have a coach, I lose focus, I get taken in by the bright shiny things and move away from my strategy.

As long as I'm running my business I will always be working with a coach.

IF YOU COULD DELIVER YOURSELF A MESSAGE WHEN YOU FIRST STARTED YOUR BUSINESS WHAT WOULD IT BE?

My message to myself would be:

"Take the leap. It's scary on the edge, but it's exhilarating when you jump, and you'll end up doing things you never even knew you could."

Laura Duggal, Life Coach
facebook.com/LauraDuggalCoaching

Author's tip: Coaching sessions take time to have an impact. Some people take immediate action, others need longer to consider the next move. Your coach will very quickly suss out what type of approach suits you – then our job is to work with that and still stretch your boundaries, by listening and asking the right questions.

CHAPTER 4
PERMISSION TO SHINE

WHAT DO YOU FEEL WAS MISSING FROM YOUR BUSINESS BEFORE YOU ENGAGED A COACH?

My life before hiring a business coach was, let's say, quite erratic. I had no real direction to focus on, or goals to achieve, as work was just a treadmill of new projects to start and finish, then on with the next, mixed with a little networking online. My working hours were also off the radar because work and leisure were blurred into one and breaks were sporadic and rare.

I had taken the bold step to mix up my life a few years earlier by reading self-help books on a range of subjects from money management, to working remotely, to decluttering and several marketing books, all of which helped to turn my world upside down in great ways. But, and this is the thing, I still had no clear direction or goals, so these were acting as exercises to free up my life but could not necessarily lead me to business happiness or fulfilment.

The mistakes I made were simply a lack of repetition and

19

planning, which are pretty essential to the success of any business. Back then, I felt exhilarated and liberated from the chains of conformity and it felt like I was on a path of random achievements that were guiding me wherever they went, instead of me having the reigns and the compass to navigate.

WHAT WAS THE SHIFT THAT GOT YOU STARTED ON YOUR SELF-DEVELOPMENT JOURNEY?

My self-development journey started about 5 years ago when myself and my partner felt that life was boring, and we had become trapped by the world around us and other people's expectations. My daughter had turned two, so family life was getting back to some level of normality, but we were both tired of our current lives. And so, we both found books of interest to us and we read them incessantly and put into practice the advice inside these.

Back in September 2016, my partner and I split amicably, realising that our own learning journey's had helped us to realise that we had different paths to follow. So, I embarked on a brave new world and a new chapter in my life.

I jumped head first back into networking to promote myself locally and gain new clients. I had a renewed sense of urgency, as I had no income to speak of, so I was pretty much working to live, with little focus on where I was heading and why. Everything was a blur really; I was taking too much time out of work to escape from it or suffering from chronic procrastination.

I'd learnt so much in a few years through reading and experiencing but I needed accountability and a guide to help me achieve success and take my business seriously again. Getting a coach was such a huge leap of faith for me, but it was instantly rewarding. I felt relief and excitement for the future.

WHAT'S THE 'ONE THING' YOU HAVE ACHIEVED THROUGH BEING COACHED?

One thing, and this is such a big thing, that I have achieved by being coached is that I had given myself permission to succeed in life and not just drift from one thing to the next. It may not seem much, but to someone that spent their life daydreaming and drifting through it, this was a complete rebirth. I had shed the skin of my past self to transform into a new person, with a new mindset.

In just one coaching session with Robin I had a plan, not just a group of ideas, but a firm plan of attack. I had a new service to offer and this new service was thrilling to think about.

There was some hesitance and a little nervousness as this was out of my normal comfort zone, but I knew that I had the right process to make it work and a healthy profit margin to earn.

Now that I had a new service in place, a new process to follow and the realisation that I was actually allowed to be successful, I knew I needed to take myself and my business seriously.

COULD YOU HAVE DONE IT ON YOUR OWN?

On reflection, I could have achieved new levels of success on my own steam from continued learning but there would have been no timescale for achieving it. My journey has been incredible with so many personal highs and I have loved every minute but there was no goal or goals for my business, as I was simply trying new things to be different and to think differently. The best part of coaching is that you have someone that holds you accountable and that is such a huge gift to receive and one that enables growth and success in any business.

If you could deliver yourself a message when you first started your business what would it be?

IF I COULD SEND MYSELF A MESSAGE, BACK TO THE START OF MY BUSINESS IT WOULD BE THIS:

"Jason, you have permission to be successful in life. Use your many talents to achieve this and don't try to do everything yourself. Find a coach that fits and go shine."

Jason Conway, Cre8urbrand - www.cre8urbrand.co.uk

Author's tip: How you feel after each session is a good indicator of the coach and your coaching sessions, but be ready for unexpected levels of emotion, both positive and negative. Coaching gives you space to evolve personally, at the same time as making progress on your business.

CHAPTER 5
CLEARING STRESS FROM YOUR VISION AND VALUES

WHAT DO YOU FEEL WAS MISSING FROM YOUR BUSINESS BEFORE YOU ENGAGED A COACH?

I had been running a fairly successful accountancy practice with 3 staff and around 300 business clients, but I had got to a point where I felt unsure about the future for the first time. I had built a practice that had plenty of new enquiries and good client satisfaction. We mainly focused on small business and keeping them on the right side of HMRC and the law. What highlighted that things weren't quite right, was the upcoming legislation changes, because I couldn't see how we were going to achieve the new requirements without changing things. I'd started changing how the practice was being run, by introducing new software and different ways of working, but I was not making progress very quickly. Time was a massive issue, or rather the lack of it. I never wanted to work crazy hours to earn the money I desired, but instead found I was working more and more just to keep afloat. My assessment was that things must have gone wrong somewhere. Had we taken on too many clients for what we could handle? From speaking to other accountants that didn't seem to be a problem. All I knew was that this was no longer fun and that there must be a better way.

WHAT WAS THE SHIFT THAT GOT YOU STARTED ON YOUR SELF-DEVELOPMENT JOURNEY?

Having always thought business and life coaches were a bit of a farce, I was convinced by one of my own clients to give a local business coach, Robin Waite, a try. Mainly because he was different and offered straight talking no-nonsense advice. This sat quite nicely with me as it matched my own approach.

One quick meeting with Robin explaining my current predicament and I left with some clear direct advice about how to overcome my problems. Some of the solutions which came up were so simple and obvious that I thought 'why had I not thought of this myself?'.

The biggest step took me a while to fully comprehend and get my head round. To deliver the level of service we wanted to, we had to increase prices, and, to existing clients too. Super scary! What if it all went wrong, and I was left with a business with no income, struggling to pay staff and bills?

I slowly set about developing packages that delivered our vision at prices nearly double of what we charged before. I tested this tentatively, but it was the loss of a major client that convinced me. I had a 'turbo call' with Robin because I was having a wobble, thinking if we are losing a major client, maybe this isn't the right decision. He made me realise that relationship might have felt like a major client, but it really wasn't, with their demands. I felt re-invigorated and made additional efforts to move forward with transitioning existing clients to our new packages with double quick speed. The positive sign-up rate went beyond my expectations.

WHAT'S THE 'ONE THING' YOU HAVE ACHIEVED THROUGH BEING COACHED?

Most of all, I have learned how to really value what I do. Previously I thought the way to achieve what I wanted, was to offer quality services, that were quick and efficient at a sensible (low) price. I was feeling the pain of trying to deliver all this and realise it's simply not possible over the long term – something has to give. I knew what I wanted to achieve in my heart and head, that was quality and speed. If customers wanted those, the price then became what would have to change to continue to achieve the other two elements.

This taught me to really seek the ideal client. If they want quality and speed but don't want to pay, then they are not for us. People we want to work with have a similar mindset of wanting to achieve quality and speed of delivery, and they recognise this needs to be paid for. Without this understanding, they will not understand us, and our relationship will fail.

We now search for the ideal client with a fantastic onboarding system. We are far more organised with a clear vision of the future. I trust in what we have done and where we are going, and I trust my coach will help me to achieve that in the best way possible.

COULD YOU HAVE DONE IT ON YOUR OWN?

No. I already had achieved a level of success; I had a nice level of income, with nice cars and a nice home. However, work was stressful, constantly chasing deadlines and playing catch up, which was completely against what I preached, but definitely what we practised.

Working with Robin as a business coach has enabled me to achieve focus. Yes, I'm taking steps backwards at present in terms of income levels, but I'm comfortable it will set in place everything for a much better future with higher income. We will have a more organised and structured working environment, which actually works how I want it to. We do now practice what we preach.

IF YOU COULD DELIVER YOURSELF A MESSAGE WHEN YOU FIRST STARTED YOUR BUSINESS, WHAT WOULD IT BE?

"Understand your key values and why you are in business. Then work this into your offerings to customers/clients. Don't be afraid to be different and to shout about it. Work this into packages that really help people how you feel they need to be helped and price yourself according to what you deliver. Cheap is not the way to grow a sustainable long-term business."

Ian Morgan, MBS Accountants
https://www.mbsaccountants.co.uk

Author's tip: A coach will help you define your personal values and support you to take on customers who also reflect those same values. It's such an important factor in how successfully the business operates, how the team manages stress and how much satisfaction or fun you can have in your business – which all lead to reaping the monetary rewards.

CHAPTER 6
THE ONE WHO DIDN'T NEED A COACH

WHAT DO YOU FEEL WAS MISSING FROM YOUR BUSINESS BEFORE YOU ENGAGED A COACH?

I started my branding consultancy kind of by happy accident – I had taken a prolonged career break from media after the birth of my second child and chosen to retrain as an Interior Designer – something I felt I could do from home and fit around the kids.

At the same time, my husband started his own business. As my first degree was in Graphic Design he asked me to create his corporate identity for him. His brochure got held up at an entrepreneurial event - the speaker told the room that this was the standard they should aim for - and he came home with seven business cards that day! I could've started an interiors business with no clients or go back to my roots and run with this opportunity. I had loads of clients at launch so didn't see a problem – yet.

What was missing from my business though, was any form

of strategy. I was making it up as I went along. I was always busy, so I didn't see a need for a coach. But I was doing that classic thing that many new business owners do of wanting to help everyone who asked me. I was also scared to turn down any business in the early days and I hadn't really identified my target client, so I wasn't necessarily working on the right type of business.

What was also missing, after three years out of work (i.e. raising two little boys) was my confidence. It's bad enough returning to an old job you know, but I'd always worked for (hidden behind?) big famous brands such as emap (now Bauer) media with e.g. Heat, Empire, Grazia, Q magazines and TV/radio stations e.g. Magic and Kiss), The Telegraph, O2 and Trinity Mirror Group.

Suddenly having to stand as myself and my unknown company was daunting – but again I was flattered that anyone wanted to pay me as an expert in anything but weaning and nappy-changing.

WHAT MISTAKE(S) WERE YOU MAKING?

To build my confidence and portfolio, I'd done a few 'mates rates' jobs for friends (as well as my husband's freebie – he has me on retainer now!) which were fine, but I didn't know when to stop! If a client said they couldn't afford me, I'd drop my price in order to help them and not lose the business. I took on any work that came my way (and lots did) but didn't have the confidence to stand my ground on things like pricing – or even charge my worth.

The biggest mistake was that I was pricing myself too cheaply for the amount of value I was giving my clients. When I worked it out as an hourly rate, I was making below minimum wage! This isn't a sustainable way to run a business but of course, your clients won't tell you that – no wonder so many new businesses don't last the first couple of years.

My worst experience was working with a client who'd said I was too expensive when I quoted him my rates at the time (they are three times that now!). I knew I could do a beautiful job for him, and it would be a creative portfolio piece for me too, so I decided to take the hit and drop my prices significantly to help him.

He turned out to be a nightmare. Clearly thinking me a pushover, he subsequently didn't value what I did, didn't listen to any advice and was determined to dislike anything I put in front of him. It was horrible, as I pride myself on really listening and meeting my client's needs, but I couldn't do anything right for him.

My confidence plummeted even further. Maybe I couldn't hack it working for myself after all? Maybe I wasn't tough enough – or, worryingly, even good enough?!

In the end, realising he was the problem, not me (as all my other clients were happy!), I wrote to him after the last load of tacky ideas he wanted working up and gave in. Yes, I would do what he'd asked for, even though I thought it was a dreadful idea, as long as he didn't tell anyone I'd done it and that if this could stand as the last work I would do for him, I'd waive the 50% outstanding fee. Funnily enough, he was happy with those designs – I reckon he'd just been griping because he never wanted to pay my full fee.

HOW DID YOU FEEL ABOUT YOURSELF AND YOUR BUSINESS BACK THEN?

I really wanted to follow my passion, and I knew I could add far more value than just a design service in terms of strategy, marketing advice and commercial, big brand experience. (I'd also studied Marketing after my Graphics degree and then worked in media, creating paid-for promotions and sponsored content-led campaigns).

However, I was frustrated at losing out to or feeling I needed to compete with other 'pure' designers, who inevitably were cheaper than I was. I saw high-street printers and copy-shops charging tiny amounts for awful logo designs and I knew I did not want to swim in those waters.

I knew was better than that, but how to differentiate myself? And that lack of confidence was a killer: why would anyone hire me over all the 1000s of other cheaper options out there?

I also really didn't know how I could make a sustainable and scalable business without burning out and whilst also being a present mother to my two young boys.

WHAT WAS THE SHIFT THAT GOT YOU STARTED ON YOUR SELF-DEVELOPMENT JOURNEY?

I love learning new things and challenging myself in different ways, so I have always tried to learn new things all the time, all with varying degrees of completion and success. Not limited to business, this has included learning to ski only 10 years ago, Interior Design (I finished that degree and got a first!), Spanish (I got conversational, rusty now), French (ditto) and coding (gave up, found a coder instead!).

I knew I needed professional help to fill in my MANY knowledge gaps, so having read one of Daniel Priestley's books 'Key Person of Influence' and seen the transformation to my husband's business, I enrolled on a course run by DENT to learn the basics of running a business, scaling up and standing out. Through that course, I was put into contact with Robin Waite – an ex-alumni - who was at the time relaunching himself as a business coach.

Serendipitously, he needed some design work done, but instead of accepting payment, I asked to be coached by him. I knew that having another person 'in my business' would be far more valuable to me than cash!

I was, of course, right. Within our first session, Robin had poo-pooed my pricing, telling me I should double – no TRIPLE – what I was charging as I'd been massively underselling my services. I would have simply never got the balls to do that by myself.

As I was also moving into a new industry, albeit one I'd trained for decades earlier – I was having to re-establish my credibility to a new crowd in a different space to where I'd been before. Robin helped me massively with giving me the confidence to believe that yes, I could do this and gave me various strategies to help me manage my time more effectively around my children too.

WHAT MOMENT TRIGGERED YOU TO THINK, "I NEED TO DO SOMETHING DIFFERENT RIGHT NOW OTHERWISE NOTHING IS EVER GOING TO CHANGE." AND WHAT DID YOU DO?

I think it was the bad experience with the property guy I mentioned!

I signed up for the DENT course and then sessions with business coach Robin! Working with Robin set off a train of thought; my assistant and I soon realised that branding for entrepreneurs wanting to grow their business was where we could really make a difference. This was our target market!

HOW DID IT MAKE YOU FEEL?

That suddenly it wasn't just me, floating around with no particular direction or accountability. It boosted my confidence that I was indeed doing the right thing, that I COULD make a difference, I WAS good at what I did and that I COULD make a living out of it!

WHAT'S THE 'ONE THING' YOU HAVE ACHIEVED THROUGH BEING COACHED?

It's added huge amounts of value. My revenue year-on-year has gone up 33%; at the same time, I've doubled my profit. Most businesses don't make a profit in their first year, so I'm proud of that.

It's not the vast sums of cash I know Robin has achieved for his other clients and that I thought I would do by just having a coach in place (I know!!!), but I have an intentionally small business which keeps me fulfilled, semi-part-time, and gets a great result for my clients. I don't have as many clients as before – but because I charge my worth, I don't need as many.

That and the time-management ideas Robin gave me (it's easy for your business to consume every part of your day, night and weekends!), frees up more time to work on my business, contribute to books like this, and I'm also a Brand Mentor for the Shifts to Success programme, helping ex and serving police officers become entrepreneurs.

I also get to spend more quality time with my loved ones. Christmas 2017 was the first time I've gone on holiday without my laptop since the kids were born – I've always been studying or working. It felt great to live just in the moment with my children – that's priceless.

I also have time to volunteer to read with the kids in my son's Reception class at school every week. It's great to feel like I'm in a position to give something back.

I don't think any of that would have been achievable if I was still running around like a headless chicken, working for peanuts.

I wouldn't do anything differently – I'm growing my business slowly and organically and it feels natural and not stressful to do it this way. I haven't got a sales funnel or process at the moment – all my business has been referral and word-of-mouth - but this is something to look at for 2018.

COULD YOU HAVE DONE IT ON YOUR OWN?

No, I wouldn't have had the confidence or been able to see the business from 'outside' to pinpoint areas to improve – or ignore: we can spend a lot of time working on the wrong things that don't make that much of a difference after all.

There's a saying "there's no such thing as a self-made millionaire" – i.e. they needed help getting where they were too! I clearly also got a bit addicted to the coaching experience: when I acquired a life coach as a client – yep – I traded my skills for hers too.

IF YOU COULD DELIVER YOURSELF A MESSAGE WHEN YOU FIRST STARTED YOUR BUSINESS WHAT WOULD IT BE?

"Get a coach. It will help you to cut the crap."

Sapna Pieroux, InnerVisions ID
www.InnerVisions-ID.com

Author's tip: Confidence always affects our decisions, but it's natural for it to fluctuate. A good coach will help you find ways to improve your self-esteem and value what you do; how this translates in business is setting your prices at the right level and aiming for the value you are worth.

CHAPTER 7
THE ETHICAL HACKER

WHAT DO YOU FEEL WAS MISSING FROM YOUR BUSINESS BEFORE YOU ENGAGED A COACH?

I didn't have a business before I engaged a coach! For a long time, I was stuck working 9-5 (8-8 in reality) in large corporate companies, dreaming about a better life and being able to run my own business. I had lots and lots of ideas for what I wanted to do but never ended up executing on any of the business ideas I had.

I would often have an idea, dream about how it would look in a few years, buy a domain name, create a website and get almost to the point of launching it before scrapping the whole thing! Looking back now, I lacked a clear plan, confidence, focus and a 'WHY'.

I had a fear of failure that was holding me back, I knew I could add value and help people, but lacking confidence is why I failed to execute.

Self-awareness was also a thing I was missing, knowing who you are, what you care about and what your strengths and weaknesses are is key to finding your passion and knowing when to seek external help, for me that was in the form of a Business Coach.

WHAT WAS THE SHIFT THAT GOT YOU STARTED ON YOUR SELF-DEVELOPMENT JOURNEY?

I hit a financial goal in my corporate career and didn't feel satisfied or fulfilled at all, I reached out to my network looking for recommendations for what I thought I needed (a life coach) but after a few taster sessions, I quickly realised that wasn't what I needed, I wasn't looking for personal development so the ideal fit for me was a no-nonsense Business Coach to educate, make me act and be accountable for what I say I'm going to do.

I had a 2-hour consultation with Robin and left feeling empowered, educated and motivated, I felt like I had a purpose, a goal and more importantly a plan on how to get there.

I've worked with Robin 1:1 ever since and haven't yet found a problem he is unable to either help me with directly or point me to the ideal person.

I'm now much more fulfilled in my work, knowing I'm helping small businesses and entrepreneurs, while at the same time doing something I love.

WHAT'S THE 'ONE THING' YOU HAVE ACHIEVED THROUGH BEING COACHED?

I've now quit my corporate job and I'm running a Cyber Security business that I love, I'm passionate about, dedicated to and I have exciting growth plans for the future.

I have more freedom with working hours and location as well as more time with family, from working smarter not harder. I have processes and use automation where it's relevant which means I can focus on delivering value and growing the company rather than on admin, all of which I've learned from Robin.

Being part of Fearless Business and engaging with the community daily is a massive benefit, entrepreneurship can be a lonely place so being able to help others and equally learn from others on a similar journey is fantastic, hearing other people's positive wins is hard when you've had a bad week can be tough, equally shouting about your successes when others are having a tough time is difficult. This does, however, get home the point that things are never as bad as they may seem.

COULD YOU HAVE DONE IT ON YOUR OWN?

I 100% wouldn't have had the focus or more importantly the accountability to make this happen on my own. Robin (and the Fearless crew) are always there when I need them which is especially important when starting on your own.

Had I not found Robin, I would still be exchanging time for money working a comfortable yet unfulfilling and boring corporate life.

IF YOU COULD DELIVER YOURSELF A MESSAGE WHEN YOU FIRST STARTED YOUR BUSINESS WHAT WOULD IT BE?

"Have a super-clear vision on who you want to help and how; "I help x to achieve x". Remember, It's all about the customer! Also, get yourself out there, meet people, network, have conversations and add huge amounts of value without expecting anything in return.

Oh, and start daily affirmations, Now!"

Chris Gough, Mintivo – www.mintivo.co.uk

Author's tip: When you've got lots of ideas, it's easy to get distracted easily and do none of them. Top coaches will always bring you back to what's important, analyse the alternatives and help you focus on a vision. Check with your preferred coach which tools they use themselves, and which books they've read and would recommend.

CHAPTER 8
FINDING THE LEADER WITHIN

WHAT DO YOU FEEL WAS MISSING FROM YOUR BUSINESS BEFORE YOU ENGAGED A COACH?

Although I'd been working as a freelance marketer and copywriter for over two years, my business simply didn't have a leader or a strategy. I thought about revenue and type of customers I wanted to work with, but like many micro businesses, I was too busy doing the doing for my clients.

I was fairly successful with sales, going to local networking and winning a new client every month. Mostly, I was hired as a copywriter because I showed lots of enthusiasm, understanding of the industry and demonstrated I knew how their marketing could work more holistically. I knew I had to focus on results for the client rather than just be a spare resource in their marketing team. But I didn't have a brochure or a website explaining my process, so it was hard to describe exactly what I could do to help the client and how it would make a difference to their sales.

The most obvious mistake I made was playing small; I didn't dare to dream about I could really apply my customer loyalty expertise to deliver marketing services because it's a very busy field. There are so many content and digital marketing experts out there! As I was working to fit around my young children, I felt "part-time" and lacked the confidence to redesign my services and price them at a market rate. Even though I was brave enough to start up, it was a big leap, because I've shied away from roles of leadership earlier in my career, preferring to be a right-hand man. I was painfully aware of several skills gaps, so went on lots of training courses to help me learn how to run a business. Even though I felt very uncertain about what my business could look like in future, I knew I couldn't go back to a regular corporate marketing job.

WHAT WAS THE SHIFT THAT GOT YOU STARTED ON YOUR SELF-DEVELOPMENT JOURNEY?

In November 2016 I pitched for a copywriting project with a small software firm; an ideal client who wanted business case studies and copywriting for their website refresh. It went well, and they gave me positive feedback but chose a writer with more tech experience. I learned two things: I needed more on my portfolio, and I was more interested in developing case studies than writing website copy. I started to explore case studies as a potential niche, researching who else specialised in it and what pricing applied.

After finding Case Study Ninja in the UK, I contacted Sarah at Case Study Ninja to find out how she worked with freelance writers. At the same time, I was looking for a business coach. I was juggling a lot as a mum, wife and business owner, but was conscious I really didn't have a plan for the business.

I still wasn't sure whether the niche would suit me or be feasible. I felt my enthusiasm bubble back up, talking about creating case studies with a couple of colleagues. An authentic client case study brings a wealth of intangible benefits. Sharing them affects confidence and culture in a business, and they work as powerful marketing content to drive website traffic, grow social media reach and increase customer engagement. I love helping other people see their success reflected in the words of their customers. At my first session with Robin, I talked about my experience and he immediately "got it". His practical questions helped me analyse the case study process takes, how many customers I could manage, and who the ideal clients were to use success stories as a marketing tool.

WHAT'S THE 'ONE THING' YOU HAVE ACHIEVED THROUGH BEING COACHED?

Before meeting Robin, no-one challenged me to set goals with my husband's input. Since doing that – talking about our income, his career dreams, my goals and what lifestyle we want – my whole mindset has shifted. I feel hugely positive about our future.

As a self-employed copywriter and marketing consultant, I found work easily with local businesses – but felt I couldn't influence their strategy. I realise now, that's because I didn't see or position myself as a leader. With a fresh mindset, I now have a niche marketing business that can grow and work in partnership with others.

With Robin's help, I'm creating a set of products to meet my clients' specific business needs. It's a more simple proposition – helping businesses drive engagement, leads and sales by sharing customer case studies in their content marketing. But the challenge is staying positive and tackling each milestone – while balancing the needs of my family.

I guess it's classic 'conscious incompetence', that frustrating stage where I can see what's missing and I'm in a hurry to fix it. Until I can invest more or seek investment, I have to be patient and progress steadily. That's where the accountability at each coaching session really helps!

COULD YOU HAVE DONE IT ON YOUR OWN?

No. There's no way I could've made these changes on my own because I didn't have enough experience of building a business and I wasn't ready to design a business strategy. I needed guidance to step into leadership, and tools to adapt my time management and strategic focus - like the default diary and 6 step sales process.

I benefit massively from the group accountability to commit to new challenges - like my first Facebook live. It's less about fear for me, and more because I hadn't prioritised my own progress and online marketing – too busy being busy!

IF YOU COULD DELIVER YOURSELF A MESSAGE WHEN YOU FIRST STARTED YOUR BUSINESS WHAT WOULD IT BE?

"Go figure out the ladder for your industry or career specialism – who are the experts and what makes them successful. Then decide where you want to be and what knowledge you need to learn to get there. Surround yourself with people who want you to get there!"

Debra Penrice, 27 Marketing
linkedin.com/in/debrapenrice27/

Author's tip: Once you have a clear goal, a coach can help you develop and lead your business from ideas into a commercial reality. Your sessions give you time to work on the business, instead of staying busy within the business. Their role as a coach is not designed to get into every detail, it is about taking a strategic look at what will help the business be more successful.

CHAPTER 9
FROM CORPORATE WORLD TO PINK PIG

WHAT DO YOU FEEL WAS MISSING FROM YOUR BUSINESS BEFORE YOU ENGAGED A COACH?

When I first set up the business 4 years ago it was all about giving me more time and flexibility to be with my family. I had just had my 3rd child and was on maternity leave. What I failed to recognise was how much time a new business that had no clients would take to become established. I soon realised I needed to be not just the accountant but the marketing department, sales department and administrator, I didn't feel that I had the funds to employ any help at that point and that was one of the biggest mistakes I made early on.

I worked all the time just to get a very small return and my time with the family was not getting better, it felt like it would be easier to go back to being employed rather than having all this stress.

In the early days I felt very alone and isolated as a sole practitioner, I had been used to working in big teams in an open plan office, I was now at home with a baby trying to grow and develop a business to replace the salary I walked away from.

The main thing that was missing in the early days was people to talk to and challenge and support me and hold me accountable to the targets I needed to set and meet, I would get distracted and go off on tangents, plus I would accept every enquiry that I received whether I wanted to do the work or not, all I could see was the monetary value at that point.

WHAT WAS THE SHIFT THAT GOT YOU STARTED ON YOUR SELF-DEVELOPMENT JOURNEY?

A turning point was when a fellow business owner invited me to a networking event which just made me feel so positive, it connected me with other business owners who were either in the same position as me or further on the journey who could offer advice and support.

Networking was something I enjoyed and was a turning point in my business, I connected with some great people who have guided and supported me on my journey. I was still dubious of having direct help as feel I needed to do it all myself but was good to have people to talk to about the good and the bad.

I have had a few coaches on my journey and all have played an important role in the growth of my business and my personal development, especially in the area of pricing my services and how to market my services as well. It has been amazing to be able to run ideas past someone not directly involved in my business and get their views on things. Finding the right coach was something that became apparent after trying a few different things.

Having a coach has held me accountable but has also challenged me to go beyond my beliefs of what I thought I could achieve. It's helped me to start dreaming big and then breaking those dreams into actions to get nearer the end result.

WHAT'S THE 'ONE THING' YOU HAVE ACHIEVED THROUGH BEING COACHED?

By having a business coach for the business, it has helped me recognise my role within the business. I thought I was the one to do the work but from having a business coach it has shown me that to achieve my targets I need to work on the business rather than in it. This was a recent revelation and I have resisted this as didn't want to burden others with what I felt I should be doing. In doing this I have delayed the progress of the business. It now feels enlightening to be doing the role that is right for the business, and for me, and employing more resource to do the work.

If I could do this again, I would start the business with a business coach right at the beginning, the business would be in a totally different place if this had happened earlier in my journey. There still would have been mistakes, I am sure, but having that person to work with and journey with has been so rewarding, and we are now achieving so much more in a shorter space of time due to the accountability and having specific actions to perform.

We have now achieved the first monetary target that we set, which feels great and have just set another bigger target which will be hard. By going through all the actions that will be needed to execute it in a coaching session, it feels very achievable, and I know that the business will be supported along the way. This is a very exciting time for us.

COULD YOU HAVE DONE IT ON YOUR OWN?

In the beginning, I felt the only way was to do everything on my own. But having been on this journey for 4 years, I have recognised that you can't be everything and asking for help is not a sign of failure.

To be honest, I don't think I would want to do this – running a business – on my own so am grateful for the people I have met on my journey and for those who are now part of the growth and development in moving things forward.

IF YOU COULD DELIVER YOURSELF A MESSAGE WHEN YOU FIRST STARTED YOUR BUSINESS WHAT WOULD IT BE?

"Never be afraid to ask for help or advice from those you trust, be confident in your skills and always be honest in what you can deliver. Build a team around you who will support and help you grow."

Lesley Shelley, ShelleyHolmes Accountancy Limited
www.shelleyholmes.co.uk

Author's tip: Developing a team is another leap for a business owner. Coaching will help you see your strengths and gaps where you need other people to help. However. Potential partnerships can cause a distraction for business owners; a good coach will help you spot the underlying reasons for wanting to build the troop around you – and offer some respite from the lonely status of working by yourself.

CHAPTER 10
DONE IS BETTER THAN PERFECT

WHAT DO YOU FEEL WAS MISSING FROM YOUR BUSINESS BEFORE YOU ENGAGED A COACH?

I had been running my business consultancy for over 6 years and although I was doing OK, I didn't feel that I was making progress. I was making ends meet but not really enjoying everything I was doing. Some of the biggest mistakes I was making were to say YES to everyone and do whatever they wanted, rather than specialise in the areas I wanted to. I would also let my clients dictate the prices they paid me, so I would often find myself doing a lot of work for less money.

When I think back, I realise now I had got myself and my business into a rut and felt trapped. I needed to make money to pay the bills, so I did what I could to get money in. I wasn't thinking long-term about how I was going to achieve my goals. I had ideas of what I wanted but didn't have a plan of how to navigate my way to get them into my life.

I knew how to run a business and grow it into a successful

multi-million-pound profitable enterprise because I had done that previously with my own restaurants, but I was dubious about doing this for others. It caused me to play down my achievements and not confidently present to new prospects on what I could do for them. This would result in me either losing a prospective client or charging them less, as I wasn't valuing my own service.

WHAT WAS THE SHIFT THAT GOT YOU STARTED ON YOUR SELF-DEVELOPMENT JOURNEY?

I had read many books on self-development, mindset, business and successful business people etc. Many times, I had thought of writing a book myself. I did start writing one in 2011, got to about 2000 words and stopped. In 2016, whilst on holiday, I read Robin Waite's Online Business Startup. Robin had sent me a copy as a giveaway on a Facebook group we were both on. I loved its simplicity, Robin had taken what could normally be a techy subject, and he cut-out the jargon and explained the processes with ease. I remember thinking "I could do this", so I emailed Robin on my return from holiday asking if we could meet up for a coffee, as conveniently, he only lived 15 minutes away.

Robin, approachable as always, agreed and we met up. I wasn't thinking at this time, I need a business coach, or I need this or that from this guy, I just wanted to ask him about his book and his journey. We chatted for about an hour and by the end of our conversation I had realised that if I was going to achieve my goals I needed some help, support and guidance.

Robin didn't try and sell me his services and in our first meeting, I think I was interviewing him as much as he was me. I came away from our initial meeting with my mind firmly set on writing a book and with Robin's background I knew for me he was the one to help me do it.

WHAT'S THE 'ONE THING' YOU HAVE ACHIEVED THROUGH BEING COACHED?

Without a doubt, my biggest achievement is writing and publishing my book, Business Recipes for Success: Four Steps to Building a Successful Restaurant and Hospitality Business. When I saw my book was available on Amazon.com for the first time I was ecstatic!

It was the accumulation of 6 months' work, I am sure you can imagine, I was very emotional and proud as were the people that had supported this journey. However, as with any journey that takes you to this high point you start to ascend with the questions of what next? Publishing the book was only the first part of the journey.

Having Robin as my coach at this point was invaluable, he had already been on this journey and had the knowledge, experience and expertise to support me going forward. Although when writing my second book, I will have learnt from publishing my first the processes I have to go through.

The biggest thing you need to ensure is that you have the support in place to keep you motivated and moving forward.

COULD YOU HAVE DONE IT ON YOUR OWN?

Yes, I possibly could have done this on my own, but it would have taken much longer, and I don't think I would have got the same results. Building a personal brand is hard and at times very lonely, so having a support network such as Fearless Business and a business coach enables you to reach out ask questions and for help when you need it. You also have the opportunity to support others when they need it and answer their questions. You're running your own business, almost within a mastermind group of highly motivated and inspirational peers, who are in a similar position.

IF YOU COULD DELIVER YOURSELF A MESSAGE WHEN YOU FIRST STARTED YOUR BUSINESS WHAT WOULD IT BE?

"Be confident in your own ability, fear less and don't be afraid to just do it. Done is better that perfect, you must take action every day to move you and your business closer to your goals."

Jonathan Butler, OutSauced Consultancy
www.outsaucedconsultancy.co.uk

Author's tip: It's easy for fear or perfectionism to get in the way of us achieving our goals, and it's natural to hesitate in business. Choosing the right coach for you means they will guide you to identify actions to take to make progress. For most, this will include a push to get you out of your comfort zone. For businesses, the best example of this is when creating new content to share your expertise: books, videos, stories.

CHAPTER 11
WHAT I GOT FROM COACHING

Although I'd had a successful career as a director of science documentaries for the BBC, I'd always been a freelancer. My life's ambition was to work for Aunty, an actual staff position at the BBC. When I was offered the job of running the interactive team at BBC Bristol I leapt at the chance, even though it meant my two little boys would have to go to nursery for 4 days a week. My rationale was that once they started school, the BBC job would fit in well with family, with flexible hours, a good pension and dare I mention it, holiday pay!

My husband and I juggled child-care for 5 years, then six months before my younger child started at primary school my whole team was made redundant.

My dreams were shattered. Aged 41, all I knew how to do was to make TV programmes, so what could I do now there was no job in broadcasting? Little did I know that far away on the East Coast of America a service called 'YouTube' was being created that would open up so many new opportunities for video makers.

Whilst I licked my wounds and considered my future, I worked as a part-time classroom assistant at the primary school, built websites and edited wild-life films. Over time, the thought of running a video production business grew and I started to attend networking events. This is where I first came across a business coach. In a room full of financial advisors, solicitors and HR, coaching fell into the category of support that my little company (employing only me) didn't require.

However, never one to turn down an offer I took Rob up on a free one-hour consultation.

I'll never forget that meeting. Rob stopped me in my tracks by asking me what I wanted for my life. Did I want to continue employing myself and fitting it in around the children, or did I have a vision of something else? Like everyone, my vision of my future was often changing with my mood and my family responsibilities and I never really talked about it with anyone other than my best friend. Now a complete stranger was asking me what I wanted to do with my life.

It felt like I was telling him my biggest secret. Would he laugh at me if I told him about the company I had been building in my head? As I described it he stood, went to the white board and drew an organisational chart.

I stared at it in horror. What me? Could I achieve that? With all those people? 'Rub it off' I reacted, it was all too much.

I kept in contact with the coach via the networking group and after a few months I felt brave enough to invest in myself and give coaching another go. At our session in December 2013 I was getting busy with a number of clients, too busy to do all the work myself.

This is when Rob introduced me to the wonders of open-questioning. He opened with:

What are you going to do about that?

Well, I could take someone on to help out…

How will you do that?

Well, I suppose that I'd have to put out a job ad….

Where will you do that?

I guess the Bristol Media website is a good place to start

And when will you do it?

Well, I need someone to start in January

So when will you send me the job ad for me to check through

This week? (in a tiny voice!)

Once I'd taken these enormous steps Rob did all he could to make the recruitment process easy for me. He offered his office for the interviews, advised me on the questions and gave me a psychological profile test for the candidates. Then on interview day he showed the candidates in.

From the interviews, I took on both James and Joseph in 2014 and I'm delighted to say they are still with Skylark Media and have been a vital part of its development. I believe this is one of the most important steps in building a company. Once you commit to employing people you are taking it to the next level. From now on you're not alone, yes, there's more responsibility, but that's more than offset by the rewards of being part of a dynamic team.

Now when I meet people at networking who tell me that they are considering starting up a company, the first question I ask them is 'have you got a coach?'. If you are thinking of investing your time in a company, then the first thing to do is to invest in yourself.

IF YOU COULD DELIVER YOURSELF A MESSAGE WHEN YOU FIRST STARTED YOUR BUSINESS WHAT WOULD IT BE?

"I'm not sure that I'd be where I am now without Rob. Because he listened and allowed me to articulate my dreams I have been able to build Skylark Media. I have turned that white-board organisational chart that once terrified me into a reality that brings me immense pride every day. "

Jo Haywood, Skylark Media
www.skylarkmedia.co.uk

Author's tip: Practical help is part of any good coaches' toolkit. We have specialist skills, our little black book of contacts or some can lend a physical office space. Check what's on offer with your preferred coach – often they will add value way beyond the sessions.

CHAPTER 12
WHO NEEDS A GURU ANYWAY?

WHAT DO YOU FEEL WAS MISSING FROM YOUR BUSINESS BEFORE YOU ENGAGED A COACH?

I have always thought that I can do it on my own. I am intelligent, I have a reputation in my industry and my field, and whenever I have put events and courses on in the past, they have always done well with minimal marketing.

I then had a life shift where I moved from Hertfordshire down to the southwest of England. In some ways, I had to start from scratch again with what I was doing, and I had got to the stage in my life where I realised that I had to take things seriously and establish my businesses.

What I realised is that I needed guidance if I wanted to scale up, to turn my side business into a real business.

I was busy being busy, and I just was not actually getting anything substantial off the ground. Some events would sell out, whilst others had very little uptake. I was terribly inconsistent with what I was doing.

I didn't feel I was running a business, rather it was this thing on the side that I did, that made me some extra cash. It felt like I was running on luck, rather than being driven by intention.

The greatest challenge I experienced was staying focused and getting things done.

WHAT WAS THE SHIFT THAT GOT YOU STARTED ON YOUR SELF-DEVELOPMENT JOURNEY?

When my partner moved in with me, we were literally starting from scratch. We had both left our previous relationships to be with each other and walked away with nothing. My partner had also been through open heart surgery, and we both realised that I was going to be the main breadwinner in our relationship. This was when we sat down and looked at who I was, what I have done in the past, what I still do, and what we both could do. We then formulated our vision for our future together and realised that we have to make it happen.

We sought the help of a business coach. I knew that in the past, I had tried to "do it on my own". I would do some online course to help me, but I just never did the work. I had a vision and I needed someone to help me get there. So, I knew I needed the accountability that a coach would bring.

We went into our first coaching session not knowing what to expect. I came away with direction and a to-do list (I like to-do lists), which meant I knew what had to be done. It really felt as if a weight was lifted off my shoulders, and there was now a light at the end of the tunnel that I follow.

WHAT'S THE 'ONE THING' YOU HAVE ACHIEVED THROUGH BEING COACHED?

We started off with launching two village hall yoga classes in the area. Within a month, they were fully booked. We went on to launch two more classes and were soon running at 80% capacity. One thing led to another and three and a half years later, we now have a boutique yoga studio. In addition, we run yoga teacher training courses, retreats in the United Kingdom and abroad. We are now in the process of launching a new programme for women, and I know that working with a coach will mean that it will happen.

It really gives a sense of accomplishment and pride when you look at what you have achieved, especially in a relatively short period of time. It also fills me with a sense of excitement of what the future holds.

COULD YOU HAVE DONE IT ON YOUR OWN?

No! As I have mentioned previously, we started with a coach, and then we thought we had it under control and stopped our sessions. Big mistake. Our businesses started to stagnate. I am certain that if not for coaching, our businesses would not be where they are today. In yoga, a Guru is someone who banishes darkness, or, ignorance. An Acharya, on the other hand, represents a system and is a role model. An Acharya answers your questions, guide on the path, helps you get out of the maze, makes you understand how to move about in the world. Whilst we all need someone to shed light some light on our business and on ourselves, I feel as business owners, what we also need is someone to guide and direct us. That, to me, is what a good coach does.

IF YOU COULD DELIVER YOURSELF A MESSAGE WHEN YOU FIRST STARTED YOUR BUSINESS WHAT WOULD IT BE?

"Do not be so stubborn and just get yourself a coach. You may get to where you want to go by scrimping and saving money and attempting to do it yourself. In reality, it will take you much longer, and chances are, you will still be stuck where you are five years down the line."

Ann-See Yeoh, My Kind of Life
www.mykindof.life

Author's tip: Celebrating how much you've done already helps accelerate your plans. A coach will help you be proud of what you've achieved because they offer perspective. Then you are more able to stay positive and keep moving to achieve more than you think is possible.

CHAPTER 13
NEWBIE

I didn't double my turnover – yet.

I didn't completely change my life – yet.

I am in the process of becoming better businesswoman - now.

I am coaching newbie.

Even when I was still employed, I knew that one day when I have my own business, I would have a coach. I could always see the benefits of being coached. And all the people to whom I ever spoke about it and had a coach said the same thing - "I wish I done it sooner". I didn't want to be the person who says "I wish I did it sooner". Thus, when I have moved from safe zone of being employed by somebody else and just having a part-time business on the side and actually started my business full time, I decided to invest in a coach. It was scary and I think I am still scared. I worry that for some reason it will not work, that maybe I am un-coachable, that maybe my business is destined to fail - all the usual nonsense of self-doubt and lack of confidence.

Choosing a coach wasn't hard for me. I knew that it would be Robin straight away, call it gut feeling. I saw him several times presenting – he made sense when he talked, I've read his books – they were down to earth, with some challenging ideas but not going overboard with it. I think I never really considered anyone else. I think, if you are reading this, you most likely know what sort of person you want as a coach. You know, THAT person that can kick your ass, but not bruise you for life.

Before I started being coached by Robin, I would try to offer my clients all the time in the world, be available whenever they were available. I was working 5-6 days a week but in reality, I only had enough paying clients to work two days. On a retrospect, it was a little bit crazy. Imagine me, running back and forth to see clients and then go back to cook dinner and then don't eat that dinner because I had to see another client. MAD. It is especially strange, as I thought that time management was a skill that I possessed, after all, I was able to spin all those plates in the air and nothing broke. I was still a good mother, I worked and brought money home, paid the bills, I even had time to volunteer and have a regular massage. I was doing all the right things but not the right way.

One of the first things that I got out of being coached was sorting out my diary. I now have days when I work with my clients and days when I am at home and can either do admin work or simply do my own things. Sorting out my diary and establishing working days and days when I am not at work created this crazy thing in my diary – BALANCE. I actually have time for me now. I haven't figured out what productive things I am going to do with those home days, at the moment I use them to post content on social media and connect with people, create plans for the future. I am trying to make new friends and catch up with the old ones. I now laugh at people when they say that they don't have time to do something. You always have time, but you choose to use it (or waste it!) somewhere else.

Having a coach for me is a continuation of my self-development journey. I read many personal development books, listened to audiobooks and watch TED talks to greater my understanding of business.

All that is great but what is even better is when you have someone who can support you and help you figure out which of these brilliant ideas of yours are worth perusing, someone who can help you make scary steps and someone who is going to be there to support you when things are not going so well.

Being coached by somebody, a stranger, is not always easy. You have to do all the homework (yep, when you coached you get homework!), you actually have someone who is going to check if you called all these people that you said that you are going to call.

If you are self-employed and have no one that works with you, you purely rely on your willpower to ring your prospect, to organise the event to invite people to it. Having someone (a coach), who is not your friend or other half, to whom you can regularly communicate your successes and failures is an amazing way of starting to think clearly, saying goodbye to excuses and as Nike says it "Just DO IT".

Just do your business, focusing on what you are good at and

earn money. We are not in the business because it is a hobby of ours, we are in it to pay bills and cover guitar lessons for our children or whatever other goals you may have. If you are serious about business, you should seriously consider coaching.

"Coaching helps you to move past obstacles quicker and reach your full potential as a businesswoman or businessman."
Magdalena Lorynska, Wellness in Motion
wellnessinmotion.co.uk

Author's tip: Simple changes can make the most difference. When you have a good coach on your team, they hold the space for you to decide what to focus on, and the steps to get there. Most of all, they can act as a sounding board to keep you moving forward.

CHAPTER 14
LOOK AT THIS ROLLER-SKATING CAT!

At the start, we thought we had it sorted. We knew what we wanted and how to achieve it. We were wrong. After 1 year of 'getting by' with our new family business, we had a feeling that we could do better.

Our lack of confidence meant we tried to shake that feeling off and convince ourselves that the direction we were going in was fine, but we were continually perturbed by seeing other web designers offering much less and charging far more. They looked super successful with it too!

Compared with how hard we were working, it didn't seem right. Or fair. But we didn't know how to level up, compete, or even exceed these other businesses.

We felt stuck because we didn't want to compromise the quality of our websites or aftercare (by instead just doing a slap-dash job and charging the same), but on the other hand, we didn't know how to go about charging more for what we were providing. We were also offering too many different services. But we were too scared to change anything about how we were running things. What we were doing was just about working, so why rock the boat?

Over the first year, we had both been dipping in and out of a few books promising 'the key to business success' to try and work out what decisions to make for the best. Reading was a cheap and safe option for self-development. If an idea looked a bit scary we'd skim through that part under the naive assumption that it wasn't meant for the likes of us.

Online Business Startup was on our reading list as we'd noticed various good reviews on social media. The offer of a free Skype consultation following meant we had nothing to lose. That consultation changed everything. In the simplest of terms, we discovered 3 key things during that call;

1. our goals,
2. what we were doing that would actually help us get there, and
3. what we needed to stop doing immediately.

We finally had some clarity and focus. Something we hadn't even realised we seriously lacked. Robin now had us thinking about recurring revenue. That very evening we drew a big black line through 'logo design' on our services list. Not because we couldn't create them (we had superb feedback), but because we could clearly see that it played no part in our future business plans.

It also in no way contributed to our (newly identified) goal of creating recurring revenue. Then why were we offering it? Well, we thought 'if people are willing to pay us for it then why not?'. Now we could see why not. And we were also able to identify other work that didn't help us move towards our goals at each next step moving forwards thereafter.

This newfound knowledge shook us up. What the hell were we doing? How did we not see this for ourselves? And if we hadn't noticed this small yet, in hindsight, blindingly obvious problem in our business model, what else hadn't we seen? We knew the same day that we needed help with our business. We knew we couldn't afford it. But we also knew we couldn't afford not to.

We took a leap and trusted in Robin's experience. In 6 months our turnover had trebled. We had gained the confidence to increase our prices and were actively saying 'no' to work that didn't contribute towards our business goals, and to work that we just plain didn't enjoy doing...even when there was cash waiting.

We felt liberated and empowered.

Now, every client is on a Website Care Plan, we've attracted new monthly retainer clients, have streamlined systems and processes in place, and standalone SEO services and logo design are a distant memory.

We're even attracting Website Care Plan clients for those who have not used us for their website build. We never imagined anyone would want that at the start!

We were thinking so small. Too scared to think bigger.

We're so happy and proud to have created a sustainable and profitable business. None of these actions would have happened if we were thinking and planning on our own.

In a few short months, Robin stripped away the fog, confusion, anxiety and uncertainty that perhaps eventually we would have worked through in our own time. Confidence may have been gained from learning gradually through experience (and reading 100s of books) and the bank balance may have slowly crept up. But who's got time to wait for that? We've got little mouths to feed and a mortgage to pay for. And the eldest wants a cat!

Our boost in confidence, clarity and drive has brought about new challenges for us and our anxiety has gone up in some new respects. We are constantly stepping out of our comfort zone, so it's bound to. We're taking more risks, so we accept that. We chose that. We don't want a coach to just sit and chat about where we are; we could do that with friends for free. We want an expert to push us and guide us to where we want to be, with the assurance that someone will be there telling us what to do if it all goes wrong.

IF WE COULD SEND AN EMAIL TO OURSELVES AT THE BEGINNING OF THIS AWESOME JOURNEY, IF IT MADE IT THROUGH THE SPAM FILTER, IT WOULD READ:

<u>To: Amy and Richard</u>

Subject: Look at this roller-skating cat!

"Now I've got your attention...

Guys.

I know you're doing OK. You can't see it right now, but you really can have more.

Just because you are experts at WordPress and web design, does not make you experts in business."

Amy and Richard, Anorak Cat Web Design
anorakcat.co.uk

Author's tip: Distractions appear in everyone's diary. Coaching sessions are invaluable for stripping back the to-do list by putting some into a NOT-DO list. When you hire a business coach, find one with enough experience to help you through the big and small decisions. They'll be there to help you learn to trust yourself – and to ask for help when you need it.

CHAPTER 15
IF YOU'RE FEARLESS, ALL IS TAMED

Go dream
with all your might
rock the very fabric
of existence.

Let aspirations
charge the universe
with a shimmering sun
of abundance.

Be contagious
with radiant positivity
bathe in the certainty
of self-belief.

Banish vampires
that drain pure joy
back to shaded pits
of woe, beneath.

For anything
will be possible
if you freely believe
in yourself.

Knowledge will
unlock your potential
so immerse your hope
in the ink of wealth.

Free dive
head first and eyes wide
into lucid pools
of endless possibility.

Magnetise
your soulful mind
with adaption
and agility.

Shine brightly
and let the mystical
wings of change
flock to your flame.

Gift gravity
to spirited notions
in search of
primed hosts.

Set sail
for the truth
and ride your journey
to bountiful coasts.

For life
is a blessing
so take flight
and stake your claim.

Go catch
that fabled dragon
for if you're fearless
all is tamed.

Jason Conway
www.jasonconwaypoetry.co.uk

NEXT STEPS

There are a number of ways to take your next steps after reading this book, first and foremost check out Robin's website for his latest updates, events, and The Fearless Business Coaching Programme:

https://robinwaite.com

You can also email Robin personally at robin@robinwaite.com with any questions you might have about Take Your Shot.

It is essential if this book has inspired you even a little bit, to take action in your business. My goal for the book was to help to change the perceptions of your own business and to start the journey of change with your business. Because let's face it, nothing is going to change if you keep on doing the same old thing.

*** REVIEW OFFER ***

If you feel this book would help someone else, 1 would like to invite you to leave a review on Amazon to help spread the word about Get Coached.

If you leave a review of Get Coached and send me a screenshot or link to your review, I would like to offer you the Fearless Business eLearning course for **FREE** (normally £195) to help you Get Coached with your own business.

I've helped business owners double and treble their income, and I would love the opportunity to be able to help you do that too.

But, most of all, thank you for taking the time to read Get Coached. If I've even initiated the smallest light bulb moment in you, I have achieved my goal with the book.

ABOUT THE AUTHOR

The first job I took was a paper round, the longest one in the village I lived in, and it paid the most amount of money. The tips I collected every Christmas for four years were bigger than any of the other delivery boys and girls. It meant I could afford to buy two or three CDs a week whereas most of my peers struggled to afford one or two per month.

Soon I was investing my paper-round money in second-hand CDs and selling them at my school to my peers so that I could afford the latest albums and the best Sony hi-fi I could afford.

Not knowing what business I wanted to start; at 18 I worked as a systems analyst, which gave me an enormous insight into systems and processes but my methods resulted in staff in the company I worked at being made redundant. The money wasn't great, so by 22, I'd started a great sideline selling grade-B laptops. I made enough money to quit my job and, in one summer, made over £40,000. Mostly cash (declared, I might add) but that money was sat on the end of my bed. I did what any savvy 22-year-old would have done and bought a car, and booked a holiday with my girlfriend to Florida to see her brother.

While out in Florida I got a call from an old colleague to start up a creative agency.

My design agency wasn't like any other; ordinarily, a new client would submit a request-for-quote, which would trigger this game of "design agency ping-pong." This involved months of back and forth between the agency and customer. I knew there had to be a better way than doing everything remotely; so I created a series of intensive 1-to-1 workshops.

The workshops involved the client working directly with a strategy expert and either a developer or designer – depending on whether it was a website or branding workshop. Typically, this would take 1-2 days.

Logo design, for example; is a process which can take up to eight weeks to create a professional logo. This lengthy process is down to poor communication or lack of time. We charged £60 per hour, and a logo might generate 8-10 hours of chargeable work during that eight-week game of design agency ping-pong.

I invited the client in for a one-to-one, 1-day branding workshop. The process had seven steps with clearly defined outcomes. We charged a fixed price which was £1,495, nearly three times the hourly rate previously charged. I offered a 100% money back guarantee. I did the same with websites and created a 2-day prototyping workshop. It started to slot into place.

Four years later.

After speeding down Frocester Hill at 50+ mph, I split off from my cycling club buddies and found myself stood next to a railway line. All I could think was, "I want more, I want to go faster!" A train whooshed past. My thoughts turned to, "What if I had stood in front of that train?" quickly countered by, "Well, I wasn't! So, something had to change." – I realised that something was missing in my life and I had to act.

After talking things through with my life coach, Michael Serwa, we realised that I wasn't passionate about building websites or designing logos, I had created a "job" for myself. However, I loved working with people, teaching them, creating products for them, building assets, and creating systems so they could charge more.

Michael said to me during one session, "Robin, it sounds to me like you're coaching!"

I spent three months rebranding and relaunched myself as a business coach. I had set a goal. I wanted to get ten clients within my first year. I created 14 clients in 6 weeks. At the age of 35 I am now running a 6-figure coaching business with great clients, and it is thanks to Michael, my coach, for kicking me into action and giving me the belief that I could do it.

Now, I coach other businesses owners and managers to do what I did. My niche is professional service businesses. From creative agencies turning over £20k+ per year to large accountancy firms turning over £2m+. I have created a number of my coaching tools to facilitate my fortnightly or monthly meetings with my clients.

I get a tremendous sense of achievement when I see my clients' businesses prosper and I have a goal to help 10,000 business owners in the next five years to double their turnover within six months using my tools. I can't do this all on a one-to-one basis, so I have created a number of coaching tools and programmes, and deliver regular talks and workshops to enable me to achieve my goal.

http://robinwaite.com

FEARLESS BUSINESS

Fearless Business is for anyone who is serious about growing their business, and potentially doubling your turnover and profit within the next 6 months.

But...you will become part of a family where I am the mother hen - I am incredibly proud of my brood whenever they have amazing wins, and lightbulb moments!!!

There are a number of things you will get access to:

- Weekly 2 Hour Webinar Panel Q&A
- Access to Discounted Breakthrough Sessions
- The Fearless Business Course (worth £195)
- The 7-Day Fearless Challenges (worth £95 each) once per month
- Accountability in the Fearless Business Group
- Message me anytime you like (don't take the p*ss) with you challenges and I'll jump on it ASAP.
- Online Business Startup Course (worth £30)
- Copies of Online Business Startup and pre-release copies of my next two books, before anyone else.

- Access to my little black book of contacts

You can apply to join at any time.

Fearless Business is ONLY £47/mth. And by application ONLY:

http://fearless.biz

That's priority access to me for only £47/mth which is an absolute bargain IMHO.

Interested??? Get online and apply.

READING LIST

Title	What It's About
Think and Grow Rich Napoleon Hill	We can learn to think like the rich we can discover wealth and success.
Built to Sell John Warrilow	Creating a Business That Can Thrive Without You
Go For No Richard Fenton and Andrea Waltz	Yes is the Destination, No is How You Get There
The Startup Coach Carl Reader	Other books help you talk the talk; the Teach Yourself Coach books will help you walk the walk.
The Lean Startup Eric Reis	How Today's Entrepreneurs Use Continuous Innovation to Create Radically Successful Businesses
The Prosperous Coach Steve Chandler and Rich Litvin	Increase Income and Impact for You and Your Clients
How to Be F*cking Awesome Dan Meredith	A kick up the backside to finally launch that business, start a new project you've been putting off or just become all round awesome.
24 Assets Daniel Priestley	Create a digital, scalable, valuable and fun business that will thrive in a fast changing world
The Phoenix Project Gene Kim and Kevin Behr	A Novel About IT, DevOps, and Helping Your Business Win
Principled Selling David Tovey	How to Win More Business Without Selling Your Soul
Elon Musk Ashlee Vance	How the Billionaire CEO of SpaceX and Tesla is Shaping our Future
From Good to Amazing Michael Serwa	No Bullshit Tips for The Life You Always Wanted

Title	What It's About
The Goal Jeff Cox, Eliyahu Goldratt	A Process of Ongoing Improvement
The Big Leap Gay Hedricks	Conquer Your Hidden Fear and Take Life to the Next Level
Sell or Be Sold Grant Cardone	How to Get Your Way in Business and Life
Flash Boys Michael Lewis	If you thought Wall Street was about alpha males standing in trading pits hollering at each other, think again
Life Leverage Rob Moore	How to Get More Done in Less Time, Outsource Everything & Create Your Ideal Mobile Lifestyle
Online Business Startup Robin Waite	The entrepreneur's guide to launching a fast, lean and profitable online venture
Outliers Malcolm Gladwell	The Story of Success

as was Brits do

My experience of Polish Police Station
Idiott t rob a bank or pee on a monument
friend asked me to be a witness in
her case to

"Zrobione dobry uczynek"
Oddanie portfela znalezionego na ulicę
kosztuje cię nerwy, czas i trochę spokoju.
Nikt nie chce

35591268R00057

Printed in Great Britain
by Amazon